Birding hotspots in the Alentejo

Castro Verde and Mértola

Gonçalo Elias

Birding hotspots in the Alentejo

Castro Verde and Mértola

Title: Birding hotspots in the Alentejo
                              Castro Verde and Mértola
Author: Gonçalo Elias
Cover photograph: Great Bustard *Otis tarda*
                              (Pedro Marques)
Digital illustrations: C. Maria Elias
Production: C. Maria Elias
Printing: Kindle Direct Publishing
Distribution: Amazon.com

1ˢᵗ edition, May 2020

ISBN: 978-1707200122

Print On Demand

Contact: goncalo.elias@gmail.com

CONTENTS

Castro Verde

Lying in the middle of a vast rolling plain, Castro Verde forms the core of the so-called 'Campo Branco' (meaning White Field). Just like Mértola (described below), Castro Verde belongs to the Beja district and to the region of Baixo Alentejo (Lower Alentejo)

The concelho (municipality) of Castro Verde covers 569 km² and has about 7300 inhabitants. It is bordered by five other concelhos: Almodôvar to the south, Ourique to the west, Aljustrel and Beja to the north and Mértola to the east.

The landscape is almost flat and very open: there are almost no trees. A few streams flow through the area, towards the river Guadiana. There are also some reservoirs, used mostly for agriculture.

Mértola

Mértola is a charming little town on the right bank of the river Guadiana. It is an ancient settlement, with a history dating back to the Roman *Myrtilis Iulia*.

The municipality of Mértola is one of the largest in the entire country – it extends over 1293 km². Its population is similar to that of Castro Verde (about 7300 inhabitants). It is bordered to the west by Almodôvar and Castro Verde, and to the north by Beja and Serpa. East of it lies Spain and to the south, there is the Algarve.

The landscape differs greatly from that of neighbouring Castro Verde: there are more hills, deeper valleys and more scrub. The soil is schistose, and there is much less agriculture.

The river Guadiana cuts the municipality in two parts. The eastern side (left bank) is very dry. The most notable feature there is the old mine – Mina de São Domingos.

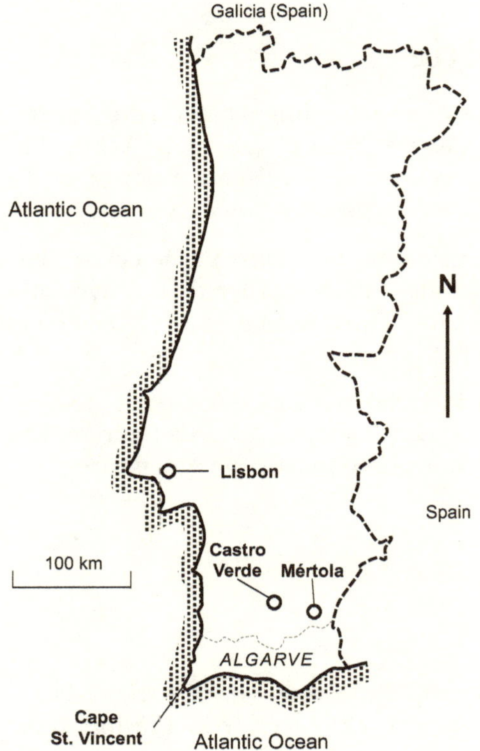

Map of Portugal showing the location of
Castro Verde, Mértola and the capital Lisbon

Birding around Castro Verde and Mértola

The region described in this book has long been known among birdwatchers as one of the best areas in Portugal for two groups of birds: on one hand, steppe birds, including bustards, sandgrouse, rollers and larks; on the other hand, large soaring birds, namely vultures, eagles, and other birds of prey.

However, the region of Castro Verde and Mértola has much more to offer, including waterbirds, passerines and other land birds, many of which are not easy to find in the country. Some highlights of this region include Ferruginous Duck, Black Stork, Lesser Kestrel, Crane, Collared Pratincole, Whiskered Tern, Gull-billed Tern, Great Spotted Cuckoo, Scops Owl, Red-necked Nightjar, White-rumped Swift, Tawny Pipit, Black-eared Wheatear, Golden Oriole, and Hawfinch, among others.

In a well-planned day visit, it is not difficult to see 70 or even 80 species, with larger figures possible at certain times of the year.

It should be noted that the area is vast, and it is not possible to explore it thoroughly in one day. The number of interesting hotspots is large and the distances are often long, so it is wise to pick hotspots that are not far from each other, to reduce travel time.

The best strategy to explore the region depends on what are the main birds of interest. Some itineraries are suggested below, each suiting a different strategy. Figures in brackets refer to the hotspot numbers – for the major sites (1 to 16), please see the map on page 13; additional sites (17 to 27) are briefly described on pages 46-48.

Steppe Birds

Steppe birds, and especially Black-bellied Sandgrouse and Calandra Larks, tend to be more active during the first hours of the day, so an early start is recommended. The best locations for steppe birds are Vale Gonçalinho (4), Rolão (5), Corte Pequena (7) and Penilhos (8), as well as São Marcos da Ataboeira (24). However, these birds can turn up at other locations, so when driving along minor roads it often pays off to stop at good vantage points and scan around. Rollers can also be found at Casével (2).

Cranes usually arrive in late October and stay until late February. The best hotspots for this species are Aracelis (6) and Corte Pequena (7), as well as Vale de Açor (25) and sometimes Fontes Bárbaras (19).

Raptors

Birds of prey can turn up anywhere, but as a general rule, the large soaring birds (Bonelli's, Short-toed, Spanish Imperial, and Golden Eagles, as well as Griffon and Cinereous Vultures) are more common around Mértola, while the smaller raptors (falcons, harriers, kites, and Booted Eagle) are usually more numerous around Castro Verde.

Considering that larger species tend to be easier to locate from mid-morning onwards, it is probably wise to start near Castro Verde, looking for smaller species, such as Lesser Kestrel, Montagu's Harrier, Black Kite, and Booted Eagle in spring or Merlin, Hen Harrier, and Red Kite in winter; resident species in this area include Marsh Harrier, Common Kestrel and Black-shouldered Kite. Good spots for all these birds include Horta da Nora (1), Casével (2), Vale Gonçalinho (4) and Rolão (5).

As midday approaches, try to move to places further east, such as Aracelis (6), Corte Pequena (7), Penilhos (8), Pulo do Lobo (13) and Mina de São Domingos (14), scanning for the larger species. Cinereous Vultures tend to join flocks of Griffons, so all vulture parties deserve careful inspection.

Waterbirds

For those interested in waterbirds, it is best to take a look at the existing reservoirs. The most interesting reservoirs are described in detail and include: Horta da Nora (1), Carregueiro (3), Rolão (5), Álvares (9), and São João dos Caldeireiros (10). In winter one can expect a variety of ducks, as well as herons and waders; in spring, typical species include Collared Pratincole, Gull-billed and Whiskered Terns (the latter one is irregular) and Little Ringed Plover. Late summer can bring a variety of passage birds, not only waders but also other species such as Spoonbills, egrets, herons and even small passerines, which are attracted to water bodies when the fields are dry and hot. It should be emphasised that water levels at the reservoirs can vary a great deal and that some of them may dry up completely in certain years, especially during the summer months.

There are other small reservoirs at the following locations: Hortas Comunitárias (18), Fontes Bárbaras (19), Entradas (20), Vale de Açor (25), Almajões (26) and Corvos (27) – please refer to the section 'Additional Sites' on page 46 for more details about these sites.

Passerines

The region described in this book is very rich in passerines, and some hotspots are particularly suitable to find them, especially in the eastern half (Mértola municipality). Great places to see a good variety of passerines include São João dos Caldeireiros (10), Água Santa da Morena (11), Mértola (12), Pulo do Lobo (13), and Mesquita (16).

In the westernmost half of the region (Castro Verde), the landscape is generally open. Typical species include larks, pipits, shrikes, starlings, Zitting Cisticola, and Corn Bunting.

Bridges are also worth inspecting, not only because they are used as a nesting site by hirundines (including Crag Martins and Red-rumped Swallows), but also because they offer the chance of getting closer to river valleys, where the thick vegetation attracts interesting birds such as warblers and chats, including the rare Rufous-tailed Scrub Robin. Please note that parking on the bridges is not allowed, so it is advisable to park before or after the bridge and walk from there.

Forest birds are not numerous, as much of the region is largely treeless. However, there are good patches of oaks along the road to Pulo do Lobo (13), at São Pedro das Cabeças (23), and around Corte Sines (27); there is a riparian gallery at Água Santa da Morena (11), a pine forest around Mértola (12) and some eucalyptus plantations at Mina de São Domingos (14). Birds that can be found in these habitats include finches, tits, Short-toed Treecreeper, Iberian Magpie, and Golden Oriole, along with some near-passerines like woodpeckers, Turtle Dove, and Great Spotted Cuckoo.

Nocturnal birds

A night visit can be rewarding, especially if the appropriate locations are visited. Little Owl and Barn Owl are fairly common around Castro Verde (the latter can frequently be found in towns and villages). Long-eared Owl is often seen roosting by day in the middle of Castro Verde town (17). Scops Owl is an uncommon summer visitor and the most reliable site is at São Pedro das Cabeças (23). Tawny Owl occurs in small numbers in forested areas. Eagle Owl is, as usual, very difficult, but the chances are higher in the eastern half of the region, for example at Pomarão (15). Red-necked Nightjar is a common summer visitor and can easily be found near Aracelis (6), Álvares (9) or Mértola (12).

Castro Verde one day

To explore the western part of the region, the best approach is to pick the hotspots closer to Castro Verde. A wise strategy is to start at locations that are good for open country passerines and steppe birds, like Vale Gonçalinho (4), and later in the day proceed to the places with reservoirs, such as Horta da Nora (1), Carregueiro (3), and Rolão (5). By mid-morning raptors should be in the air and a visit to Aracelis (6) may increase the possibility of seeing some of the larger species, with the bonus of Cranes in winter. In spring, a visit to Casével (2) may be rewarded with Lesser Kestrel and Roller.

There are several other interesting locations close to Castro Verde, please see pages 46 to 48 for more details about these.

Mértola one day

The concelho of Mértola is very large and so it is not easy to see the entire area in just one day. However, it is possible to visit the most relevant sites if the visit is planned in advance.

As suggested above for Castro Verde, it is best to start at locations that are good for passerines, namely Água Santa da Morena (11) or even Mértola town (12) and its pinewoods. After that, try to look for some open country species, namely at Penilhos (8) or Corte Pequena (7). After mid-morning, it is a great time to visit the main reservoirs, such as those at Álvares (9) and São João dos Caldeireiros (10), while looking at the sky to see some raptors. Finally, head north for Pulo do Lobo (13), looking for more soaring birds.

As to the eastern part of the concelho, the two key sites are Mina de São Domingos (14) and Pomarão (15). Both locations have a good variety of interesting passerines so an early start usually pays off. Additionally, the mine is good for White-rumped Swifts from May onwards and also for large soaring birds.

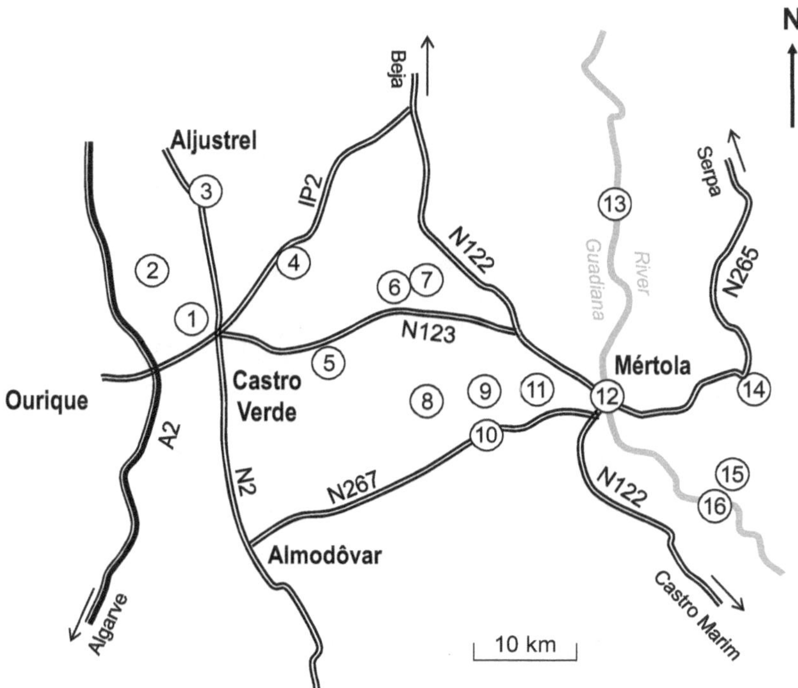

1. Horta da Nora
2. Casével
3. Carregueiro
4. Vale Gonçalinho
5. Rolão
6. Aracelis
7. Corte Pequena
8. Penilhos
9. Álvares
10. São João dos Caldeireiros
11. Água Santa da Morena
12. Mértola
13. Pulo do Lobo
14. Mina de São Domingos
15. Pomarão
16. Mesquita

Map of birding hotspots around Castro Verde and Mértola.
Only the main national roads have been drawn.

Horta da Nora

A small reservoir with good patches of emergent vegetation.

Birds

Resident: Mallard, Gadwall, Shoveler, Little Grebe, Great Crested Grebe, Cattle Egret, Little Egret, White Stork, Black-shouldered Kite, Marsh Harrier, Buzzard, Black-winged Stilt, Stone Curlew, Black-bellied Sandgrouse, Kingfisher, Hoopoe, Calandra Lark, Crested Lark, Woodlark, Cetti's Warbler, Zitting Cisticola, Southern Grey Shrike, Raven, Serin, Linnet, Waxbill, Spanish Sparrow, Corn Bunting

Breeding visitors: Quail, Black Kite, Lesser Kestrel, Little Ringed Plover, Bee-eater, Nightingale, Great Reed Warbler, Golden Oriole

Non-breeding visitors: Teal, Great Cormorant, Great White Egret, Grey Heron, Spoonbill, Red Kite, Lapwing, Golden Plover, Snipe, Common Sandpiper, Green Sandpiper, Stock Dove, Meadow Pipit, Penduline Tit

How to visit it

Horta da Nora is very easy to find: leave Castro Verde westwards on the road to Casével. About 1.5 km ahead, shortly after passing a sign reading Brunhachos and a narrow bridge, a stand of trees appears on the left-hand side. Look for a short track to the left and park.

From this point (37.7071, -8.1030) it possible to see a large portion of the reservoir. The best strategy is usually to stay here for a while, not only because of the water body itself but also because this is a convenient place from where to scan the surrounding fields. The reservoir is fenced off, but much can be seen from outside the fence.

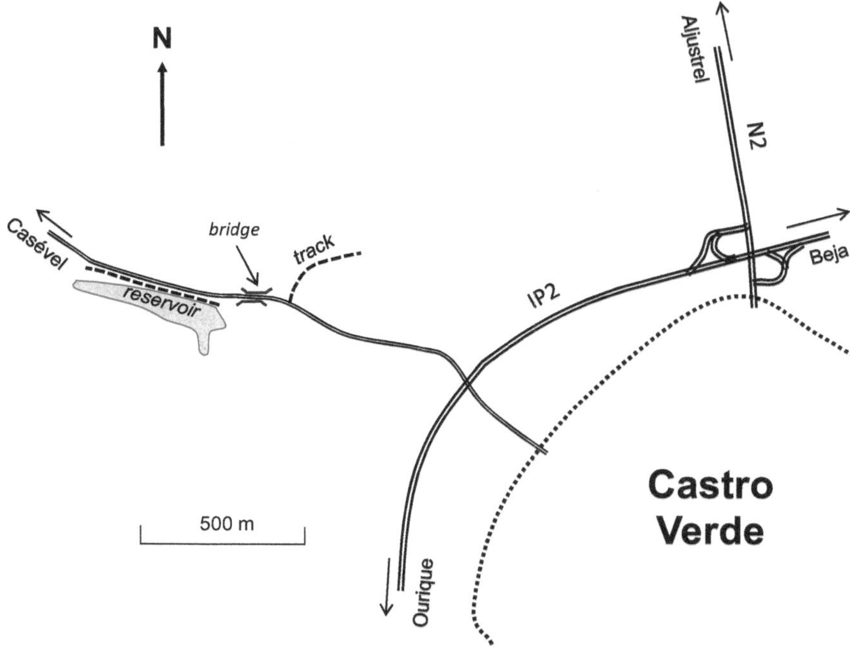

This location attracts a good variety of waterbirds throughout the year, including ducks, grebes, herons and waders. A narrow track runs along the northern side of the reservoir (outside the fence) and leads to the far end. From this track, it is possible to inspect the various sections of the reservoir. Additionally, it is worth exploring the emergent vegetation along the northern shore, which usually attracts some passerines, including Great Reed Warbler in spring and Penduline Tit in winter.

The surrounding fields hold several open country species, including steppe birds and raptors. Typical species in winter include Red Kite, Lapwing and Golden Plover, whereas Black-shouldered Kite and Stone Curlew are resident. Black-bellied Sandgrouse sometimes turns up, although it is much less numerous here than further east.

Casével

Grassland and cereal crops. An abandoned railway station is a point of interest as well.

Birds

Resident: Red-legged Partridge, Cattle Egret, White Stork, Buzzard, Great Bustard, Stone Curlew, Little Owl, Hoopoe, Crested Lark, Stonechat, Cetti's Warbler, Zitting Cisticola, Sardinian Warbler, Southern Grey Shrike, Spotless Starling, Corn Bunting

Breeding visitors: Quail, Black Kite, Montagu's Harrier, Lesser Kestrel, Bee-eater, Roller, Red-rumped Swallow

Non-breeding visitors: Red Kite, Skylark, Meadow Pipit

How to visit it

Casével is a small village about 10 km northwest of Castro Verde. Follow directions to Horta da Nora (see page 14) and continue for another 9 km until Casével. At this village, look for the road to the railway station ('estação de Casével'). This road crosses an area of open fields and leads to the old railway station, which at present is just a set of ruined buildings near an abandoned railway line (37.7794, -8.1807).

This spot is one of the best locations in the region to see Lesser Kestrels. Several pairs breed around here and are usually very easy to observe from February onwards – their calls (a quick *tchak-tchak-tchak*) are very different from those of the Common Kestrel. Roller is also regularly seen at this place, mainly between mid-April and mid-August. On top of the old railway station, there is a nest of White Stork.

The surrounding fields are worth scanning for raptors. Regular species include Black Kite and Montagu's Harrier in spring and Red Kite in winter. Other birds of interest in these fields include Great Bustard, Stone Curlew and Quail.

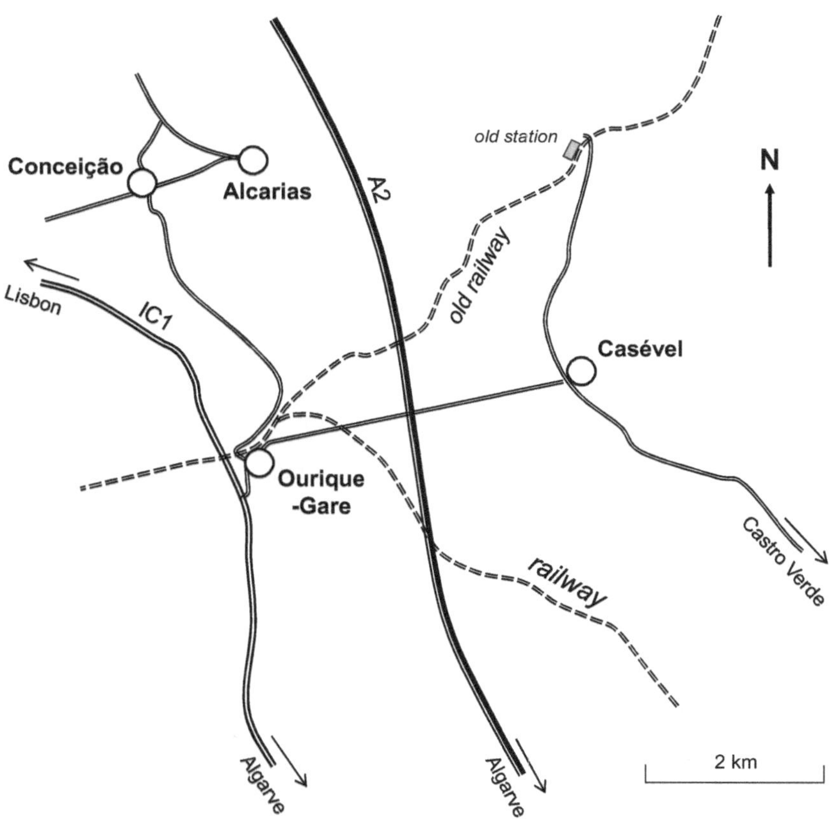

Carregueiro

Another reservoir with emergent vegetation, surrounded by pastureland and a small Eucalyptus plantation.

Birds

Resident: Mallard, Red-crested Pochard, Little Grebe, Cattle Egret, White Stork, Marsh Harrier, Kestrel, Moorhen, Coot, Little Bustard, Black-winged Stilt, Hoopoe, Stonechat, Zitting Cisticola, Southern Grey Shrike, Spotless Starling, Spanish Sparrow, Linnet, Corn Bunting

Breeding visitors: Quail, Black Kite, Booted Eagle, Little Ringed Plover, Great Spotted Cuckoo, Red-rumped Swallow, Melodious Warbler, Golden Oriole

Non-breeding visitors: Teal, Shoveler, Tufted Duck, Ferruginous Duck, Great Cormorant, Spoonbill, Red Kite, Lapwing, Black-tailed Godwit, Snipe, Greenshank, Green Sandpiper, Skylark

How to visit it

Access is from Castro Verde, following the N2 northwards for 15 km until Carregueiro. Just before entering this village, veer right on the road to Entradas and then left on a dirt road signposted 'Monte do Gavião'. This road goes through a gallery of Eucalyptus trees. Proceed for about 500 m and park (37.8218, -8.0941). The reservoir is visible on the right-hand side. It is wise to use the trees as a 'hide', to avoid disturbing the birds. In winter there are often many ducks, and it is worth scrutinising them carefully, as the rare Ferruginous Duck has been recorded on several occasions. Red-crested Pochards are regular. Waders occur at times, depending on the water level - they tend to favour muddy shores, so if the reservoir is very full, they may be absent.

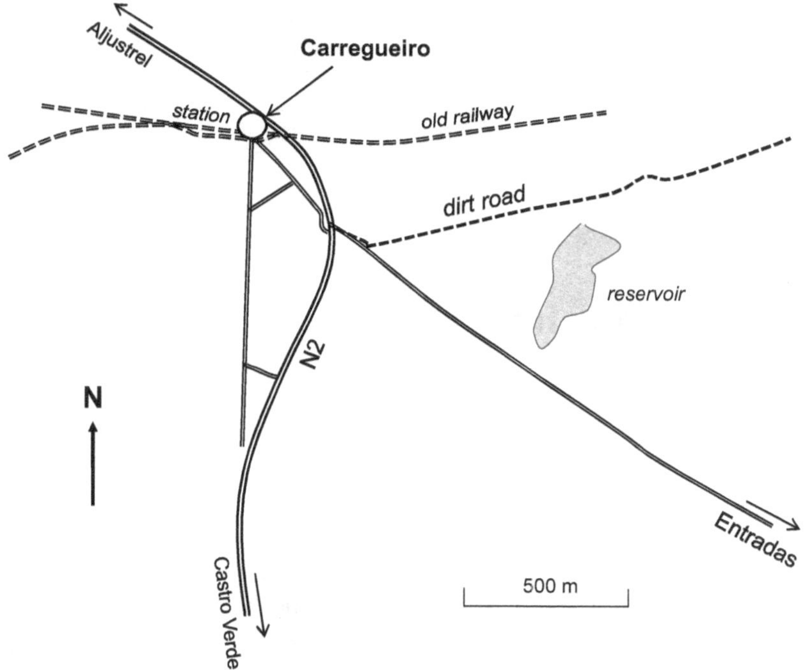

To get a better view over the eastern end of the reservoir, it is perhaps better to get back to Carregueiro and follow the road to Entradas for about 500 m. The reservoir is now on the left. This option provides a different angle and a better view of the 'upper' part of the water, especially over the muddy areas, which are now much closer.

It should be noted that in late summer the reservoir may be almost dry, and when that is the case, there may be no waterbirds at all.

Although the reservoir is the main point of interest here, it is also worth to take a look around, as there are often raptors in the sky. The bridge over the old railway attracts Red-rumped Swallows.

Vale Gonçalinho

A vast area of open fields.

Birds

Resident: Gadwall, Red-legged Partridge, Little Grebe, Cattle Egret, White Stork, Black-shouldered Kite, Buzzard, Spanish Imperial Eagle, Kestrel, Coot, Little Bustard, Great Bustard, Black-bellied Sandgrouse, Hoopoe, Calandra Lark, Crested Lark, Stonechat, Zitting Cisticola, Southern Grey Shrike, Jackdaw, Raven, Spotless Starling, Corn Bunting

Breeding visitors: Quail, Black Kite, Montagu's Harrier, Lesser Kestrel, Great Spotted Cuckoo, Roller, Bee-eater, Short-toed Lark, Tawny Pipit

Non-breeding visitors: Shoveler, Red Kite, Hen Harrier, Lapwing, Golden Plover, Skylark, Meadow Pipit, Black Redstart

How to visit it

This location lies about 5 km northeast of Castro Verde. Access is on the old N391, which runs parallel to the IP2 (from Castro Verde, look for the fire brigade and follow signs to Vale Gonçalinho). After 5 km a wide track to the right appears – a large sculpture of a Great Bustard is visible on the right-hand side. This track passes a gate which is usually open and leads to a small group of houses (37.7367, -8.0314). This is the Environmental Education Centre run by LPN. It is open from Tuesday to Saturday, and here it is possible to get some information about this location, and its birdlife. Free parking is available.

A birdwatching trail (3 km long) makes it possible to walk through the fields and to see some typical birds, including the elusive Black-bellied Sandgrouse and of course Little Bustard and Calandra Lark. In spring the male larks utter their song in flight, but in winter these birds tend to gather in small flocks. This trail can be walked on any day.

Some old buildings with holes are used by nesting Lesser Kestrels, Rollers and Jackdaws. One of them is a circular tower and it can easily be seen from the trail. There are also some photographic hides, but they need to be booked in advance, and a fee is payable to use them.

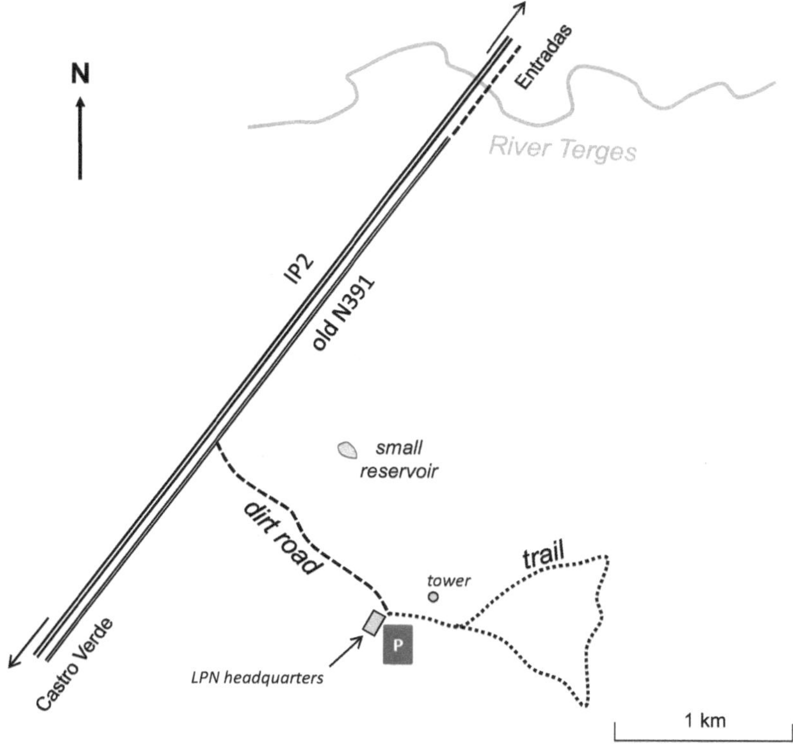

Just north of the dirt road, there is a small reservoir. It is worth looking at it, as sometimes there are a few waterbirds, including ducks and grebes. However, as it lies about 500 m away, a telescope is useful here.

Rolão

Mainly grassland, almost treeless area. There is also a reservoir.

Birds

Resident: Gadwall, Mallard, Red-legged Partridge, Little Grebe, Great Crested Grebe, Cattle Egret, White Stork, Buzzard, Coot, Little Bustard, Great Bustard, Black-winged Stilt, Black-bellied Sandgrouse, Hoopoe, Kingfisher, Calandra Lark, Crested Lark, Stonechat, Zitting Cisticola, Southern Grey Shrike, Raven, Spotless Starling, Corn Bunting

Breeding visitors: Montagu's Harrier, Little Ringed Plover, Collared Pratincole, Gull-billed Tern, Whiskered Tern, Bee-eater, Short-toed Lark, Red-rumped Swallow

Non-breeding visitors: Shoveler, Teal, Great White Egret, Spoonbill, Red Kite, Lapwing, Snipe, Greenshank, Green Sandpiper, Skylark

How to visit it

The plains south of the N123 can be inspected directly from this road; however, there is often some traffic, and cars tend to drive fast, making this option somewhat unpleasant and dangerous. A better alternative for exploring this area is along the minor road that leads to Rolão and Viseus. This road is quite narrow; luckily, there are numerous lay-bys, which can be used to stop and scan.

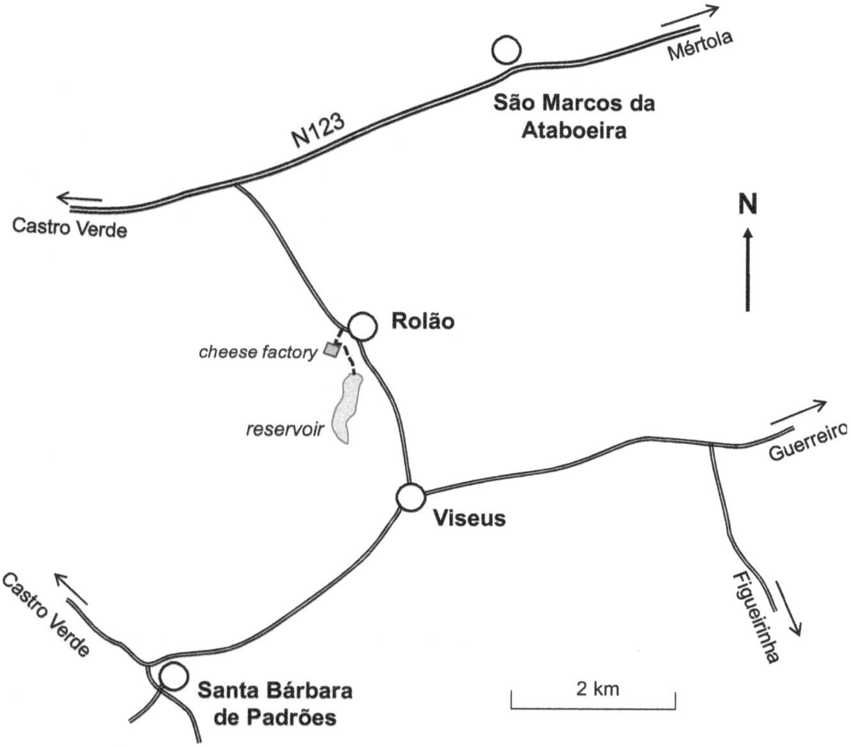

This is an outstanding area for steppe birds, especially Great and Little Bustards. Both species are very shy and do not tolerate close approach, so it is wise to scan from the car before stepping outside. A telescope is very useful here. In winter, bustards form small flocks that feed or rest on hillsides. Black-bellied Sandgrouse also occurs here.

There are fences and telegraph poles along both sides of the road, and these are regularly used as a perch by many birds, including Southern Grey Shrike and Corn Bunting.

Just south of Rolão there is a reservoir, which deserves inspection. However, as it lies on private land, permission is needed to visit it. Look for a cheese factory lying just west of the village (it has a drawing of a Great Bustard at the entrance), go to the reception (37.6742, -7.9627) and ask for permission to visit the reservoir. Access is on a rough track which can be done by car or on foot. This place is tranquil and usually has many waterbirds, including ducks, waders and sometimes terns.

Aracelis

A chapel on top of a hill, surrounded by some trees and open country.

Birds

Resident: Red-legged Partridge, Cattle Egret, Griffon Vulture, Spanish Imperial Eagle, Kestrel, Great Bustard, Little Owl, Hoopoe, Calandra Lark, Thekla's Lark, Woodlark, Blue Rock Thrush, Dartford Warbler, Sardinian Warbler, Iberian Magpie, Spotless Starling, Spanish Sparrow, Serin, Corn Bunting

Breeding visitors: Quail, Black Kite, Short-toed Eagle, Red-necked Nightjar, Bee-eater, Red-rumped Swallow, Black-eared Wheatear, Nightingale, Woodchat Shrike, Golden Oriole

Non-breeding visitors: Red Kite, Crane, Lapwing

How to visit it

To get to Aracelis (sometimes spelt Ara-Celli), leave the N123 northwards on the road signposted Salto – this minor road starts just east of São Marcos da Ataboeira. Follow it for 7 km until it starts going uphill. When a large white 'gate' appears on the left, veer right, proceed to the very top (37.7463, -7.8870) and park. It is worth climbing the stairs that lead to the chapel. The views over the surrounding plains are breath-taking.

Aracelis is an excellent spot from where to scan the surrounding plains. In winter, large flocks of Cranes are often seen in the distance, especially on the northern side. Their number can reach several hundred in midwinter. This place is also a good vantage point from where to scan for soaring raptors, especially after mid-morning.

Around the road leading to the chapel, there are a few trees, especially Eucalyptus and Pines, so it is possible to find several forest birds, some of which are not very common in the treeless plains of Castro Verde, namely Red-necked Nightjar, Woodlark, and Golden Oriole. Furthermore, the buildings here often have Blue Rock Thrush.

The 'gate' mentioned before (marked 'Herdade Vale das Covas') is also worth a stop. This is another good location from where to scan the plains for wintering Cranes in the distance – look towards the north. Great Bustards are also regular here.

Along the road to Salto, the landscape is more open and some farmland birds can be found, including Quail, Calandra Lark, and Corn Bunting.

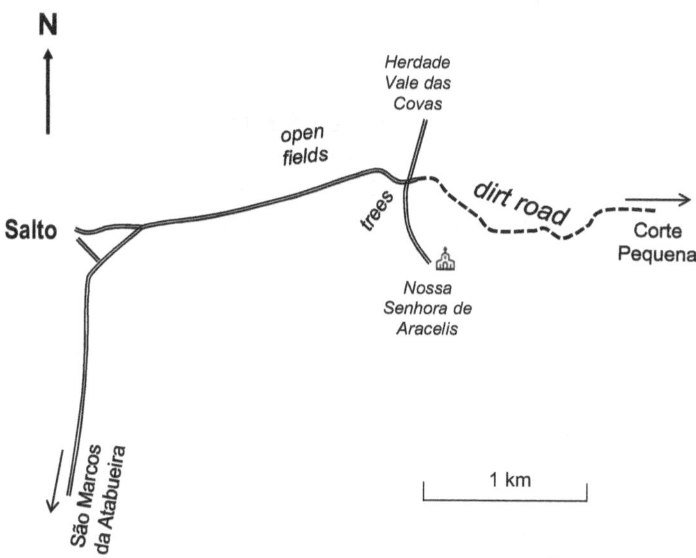

Corte Pequena

Open fields with little vegetation.

Birds

Resident: Cattle Egret, Black-shouldered Kite, Marsh Harrier, Griffon Vulture, Cinereous Vulture, Spanish Imperial Eagle, Kestrel, Little Bustard, Great Bustard, Black-bellied Sandgrouse, Hoopoe, Calandra Lark, Crested Lark, Woodlark, Southern Grey Shrike, Raven

Breeding visitors: Quail, Black Kite, Montagu's Harrier, Bee-eater, Short-toed Lark, Black-eared Wheatear

Non-breeding visitors: Red Kite, Hen Harrier, Goshawk, Crane, Lapwing, Golden Plover, Stock Dove, Skylark, Meadow Pipit

How to visit it

This area is situated north of the N123, roughly midway between Castro Verde and Mértola. If coming from Castro Verde, follow the N123 eastwards for about 20 km, then veer left where signposted 'Corte Pequena', follow this road for about 5 km and park where signs read 'Peso' and 'Balança' (37.7587, -7.8514).

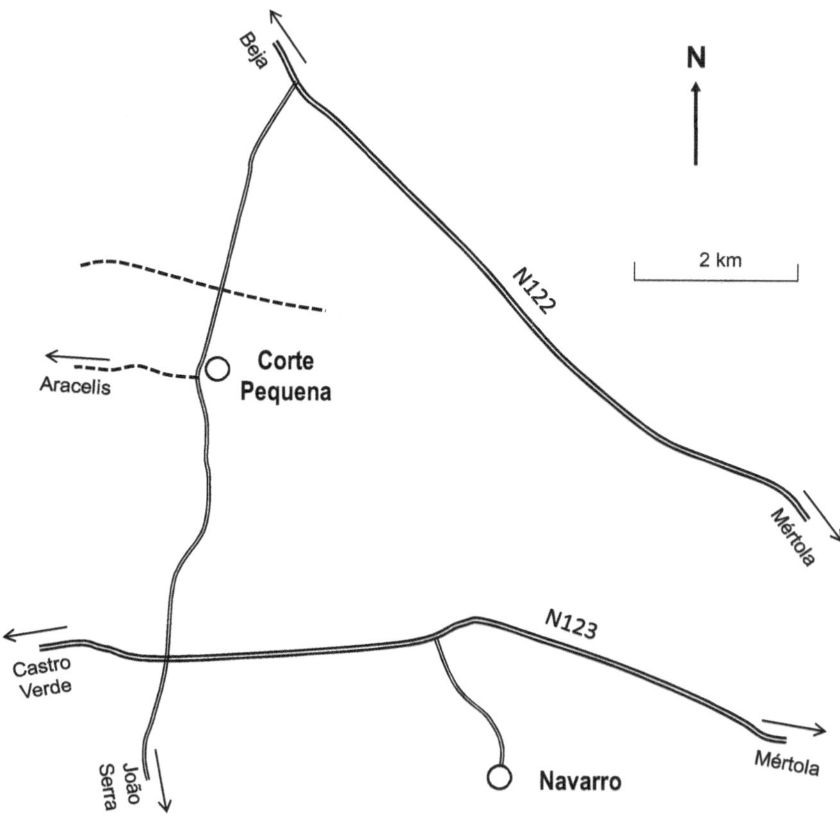

This location ranks among the best places for steppe birds. A good strategy is to stay here for a while and scan. The density of Black-bellied Sandgrouse is among the highest in the region, and these birds should not be difficult to see. Listen for their horse-like calls and look for small groups flying around, sometimes right overhead. Early morning is the best time to see these elusive birds. Great Bustards are also regularly recorded here. Small groups can often be seen on hillsides, but as usual, these birds are very shy and keep their distance. Therefore, a telescope can be very useful. Flocks of Cranes have been recorded here, and Calandra Larks are fairly common.

Corte Pequena is also good for raptors. By mid-morning it pays to stay here for a while and scan the sky. Vultures and Spanish Imperial Eagle are regularly seen here, as well as several smaller species.

Elsewhere along this road (between the N123 and the N122), it is worth stopping here and there to scan for raptors, larks and other birds. The unsurfaced road signposted Aracelis is also a good option, as it is tranquil and also provides an opportunity to see interesting birds.

Penilhos

Open country.

Birds

Resident: Red-legged Partridge, White Stork, Black-shouldered Kite, Griffon Vulture, Cinereous Vulture, Kestrel, Little Bustard, Black-bellied Sandgrouse, Little Owl, Hoopoe, Calandra Lark, Crested Lark, Thekla's Lark, Zitting Cisticola, Southern Grey Shrike, Iberian Magpie, Spotless Starling, Spanish Sparrow, Linnet, Corn Bunting

Breeding visitors: Quail, Booted Eagle, Great Spotted Cuckoo, Red-necked Nightjar, Roller, Bee-eater, Short-toed Lark, Red-rumped Swallow, Black-eared Wheatear, Woodchat Shrike

Non-breeding visitors: Red Kite, Hen Harrier, Golden Plover, Lapwing, Skylark, Meadow Pipit

How to visit it

Penilhos is the name of a village situated more or less midway between Castro Verde and Mértola, south of the N123. It lies 5 km northwest of São João dos Caldeireiros (see page 32). The area consists mostly of uncultivated land and there is not much disturbance. There is a military field nearby, but this field is currently unused.

At first glance, the Penilhos area may seem somewhat 'empty', and in fact, the number of birds around here is usually not high. However, steppe birds and large raptors are often seen at this location, and for this reason, it has been included in this book.

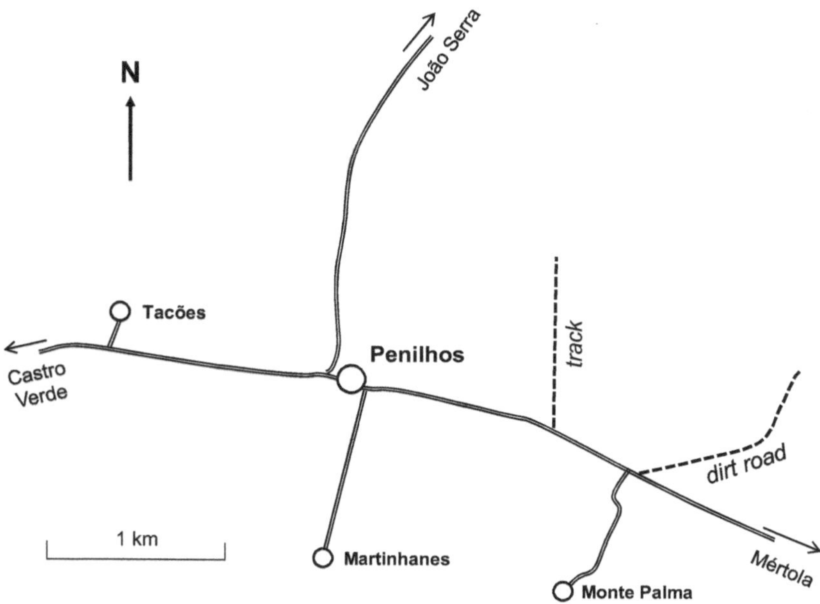

Four minor roads leave from Penilhos and any of them can be used to explore the area.

A good option is to leave the village eastwards and stop after 1 km - there is a track on the left side, just in front of a stork's nest (37.6407, -7.8385). This location is good for steppe birds, namely Little Bustard, Black-bellied Sandgrouse and Calandra Lark (large flocks of the latter are often recorded here). Flocks of Golden Plovers can be seen in winter. This is also a convenient spot to scan around for raptors, especially after mid-morning. Southern Grey Shrike is easy to see on the telegraph wires along this road.

The road south to Martinhanes also crosses some fields which attract larks and wintering Lapwings.

Spanish Sparrows are very numerous around Penilhos, they can be seen easily under the nests of White Stork, but they also nest in trees.

Álvares

Open country with some olive groves and a reservoir.

Birds

Resident: Gadwall, Mallard, Red-legged Partridge, Little Grebe, Griffon Vulture, Cinereous Vulture, Spanish Imperial Eagle, Golden Eagle, Stone Curlew, Black-winged Stilt, Black-bellied Sandgrouse, Little Owl, Hoopoe, Thekla's Lark, Zitting Cisticola, Southern Grey Shrike, Raven, Spotless Starling, Spanish Sparrow, Rock Sparrow, Linnet, Corn Bunting

Breeding visitors: Quail, Short-toed Eagle, Little Ringed Plover, Collared Pratincole, Gull-billed Tern, Great Spotted Cuckoo, Red-necked Nightjar, Bee-eater, Black-eared Wheatear

Non-breeding visitors: Red Kite, Snipe, Greenshank, Green Sandpiper

How to visit it

Álvares is located 15 km west of Mértola. Access from this town is made taking the N267 westwards, then veering right at Namorados. Proceed for another 10 km. At Álvares, look for a dirt road to the left and continue for 2.5 km until a reservoir appears on the right-hand side (37.6473, -7.8174). It is also possible to get here from Penilhos, by leaving this village eastwards and then veering left on a dirt road until the water body appears. This reservoir is the main point of interest here. The area is unfenced, and it is possible to walk along the shore.

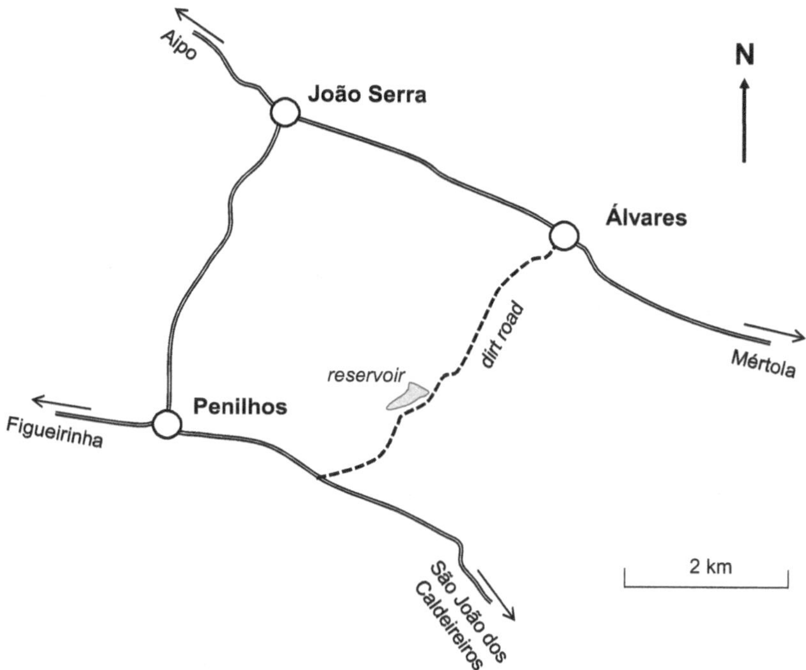

In spring there are often some Pratincoles and Gull-billed Terns, along with Little Ringed Plover and Black-winged Stilt. Other waders turn up outside the breeding season. Additionally, this place attracts other waterbirds, such as ducks, herons or grebes. However, as is the case with other reservoirs in the region, the water level can be very low at times and when that is the case there may be no waterbirds at all.

This area is also good for large soaring birds, notably eagles and vultures, so it is a good idea to scan the surrounding hillsides, especially after mid-morning. Steppe birds are less numerous here than at other places lying further to the west, but bustards, Stone Curlew and sandgrouse are seen at times. Great Spotted Cuckoo is also regular.

As to the passerines, this area is best for open-country species, such as larks, Black-eared Wheatear and Corn Bunting. As one continues westwards towards Penilhos, the dirt road is fenced, but it is possible to drive slowly while looking at the poles.

São João dos Caldeireiros

An area dominated by scrub. There is a reservoir nearby.

Birds

Resident: Gadwall, Mallard, Red-crested Pochard, Common Pochard, Red-legged Partridge, Little Grebe, Great Crested Grebe, Griffon Vulture, Cinereous Vulture, Bonelli's Eagle, Coot, Black-winged Stilt, Stone Curlew, Hoopoe, Kingfisher, Iberian Green Woodpecker, Thekla's Lark, Dartford Warbler, Sardinian Warbler, Southern Grey Shrike, Iberian Magpie, Raven, Spanish Sparrow, Serin, Corn Bunting

Breeding visitors: Quail, Little Ringed Plover, Great Spotted Cuckoo, Bee-eater, Red-rumped Swallow

Non-breeding visitors: Teal, Ferruginous Duck, Great Cormorant, Great White Egret, Red Kite, Hen Harrier, Lapwing, Snipe, Greenshank, Green Sandpiper, Song Thrush, Dunnock, Meadow Pipit

How to visit it

São João dos Caldeireiros is a small village lying about 15 km west of Mértola, next to the N267. The main point of interest here is the reservoir which lies just west of the village. Access is on a rough track that starts about 200 metres west of the village. It is best to leave the car on the roadside (37.6104, -7.7962) and proceed on foot, as this is private property. The track leads to the wall, with a good view of the reservoir.

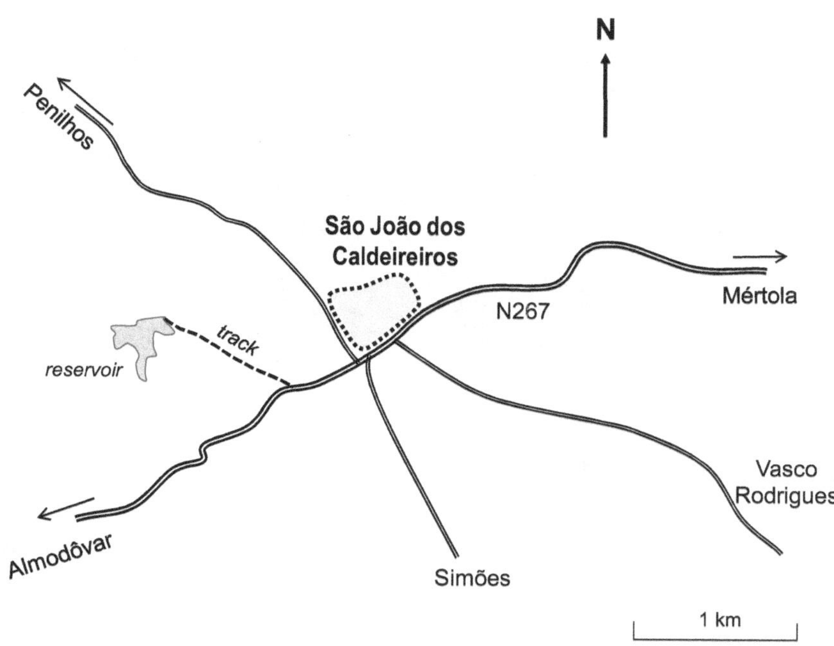

This location usually attracts a good number of waterbirds, particularly ducks (including Red-crested Pochard), grebes, coots, herons and waders. There have also been several records of Mute and Black Swans, which are probably feral, although their origin is not very clear.

The surrounding hillsides are dominated by scrub (mainly Gum Rockrose), with a few scattered trees. Along the track, it is possible to see several passerines, including Thekla's Lark and Dartford Warbler. Great Spotted Cuckoo is often seen around here and might breed.

This area also attracts large raptors, including vultures and eagles, so it is worth scanning the sky as they are often seen soaring in the distance.

At the southern edge of the village, there are some nests of White Stork, which are also used by Spanish Sparrows to build their own nests (both species may be absent in autumn and early winter).

Água Santa da Morena

The river Oeiras is a tributary of the Guadiana. At Água Santa da Morena, it forms a nice gallery with dense vegetation.

Birds

Resident: Mallard, Red-legged Partridge, Little Grebe, Wood Pigeon, Hoopoe, Kingfisher, Iberian Green Woodpecker, Great Spotted Woodpecker, Thekla's Lark, Crag Martin, Grey Wagtail, Wren, Blue Rock Thrush, Cetti's Warbler, Dartford Warbler, Sardinian Warbler, Blackcap, Long-tailed Tit, Southern Grey Shrike, Iberian Magpie, Spotless Starling, Spanish Sparrow, Chaffinch, Hawfinch, Rock Bunting

Breeding visitors: Turtle Dove, Red-necked Nightjar, Bee-eater, Red-rumped Swallow, Nightingale, Golden Oriole

Non-breeding visitors: Great Cormorant, Snipe, Green Sandpiper, Dunnock, Song Thrush, Chiffchaff

How to visit it

The easiest way to get here is from Mértola, following the N122 for 2 km, then the N267 westwards for 2.7 km and veering right where signs read 'João Serra', 'Água Santa' and 'Morena'. Proceed for 3.6 km until a bridge appears (37.6415, -7.7466). This is the bridge over the river Oeiras. Exploration is best done on foot (it is possible to park just before the bridge). This location is very rich in passerines and also has a few larger land birds.

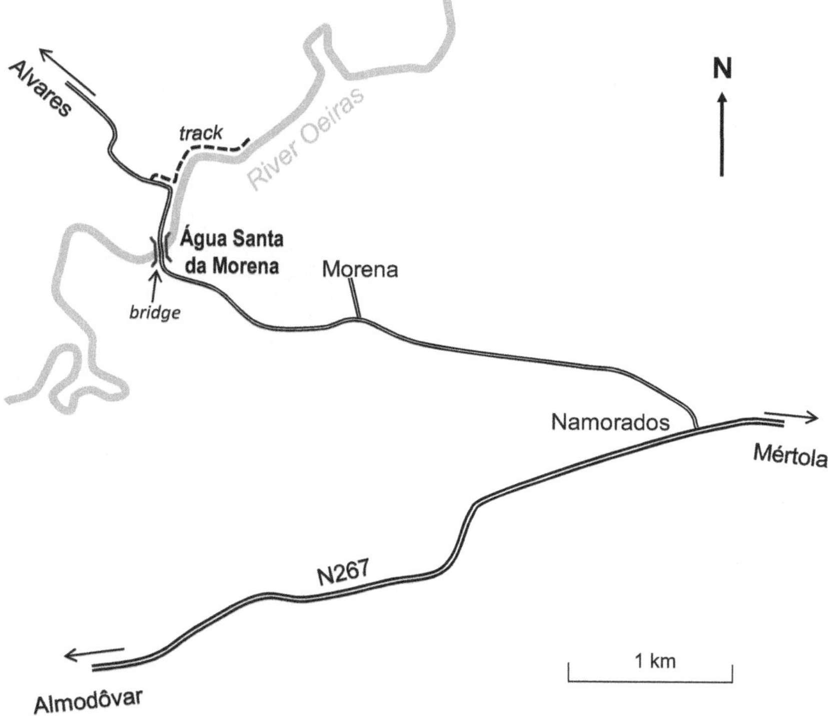

The best starting point is right at the bridge. It is worth taking a look at the river, as there are often a few waterbirds, like Mallard, Cormorant or small waders. On the other side of the road, there is an old abandoned house which is inhabited by a Blue Rock Thrush.

It is suggested to walk northwards along the road, which runs parallel to the river. After a while, there is a sharp turn to the left, and the road goes away from the river valley. However, a track to the right makes it possible to continue along the river. The slopes are covered with dense scrub, which attracts a lot of passerines, including *Sylvia* warblers, Long-tailed Tit and wintering Song Thrushes, while the larger trees along the river are favoured by the elusive Hawfinch.

Another possibility is to follow the valley to the other side. A track runs past the small houses and continues westwards along the river.

Mértola

A charming little town with a medieval castle on the right bank of the river Guadiana. The surrounding hills are covered mainly with Pines.

Birds

Resident: Red-legged Partridge, Little Egret, White Stork, Griffon Vulture, Golden Eagle, Kestrel, Wood Pigeon, Tawny Owl, Kingfisher, Hoopoe, Crag Martin, Grey Wagtail, Stonechat, Black Redstart, Blue Rock Thrush, Cetti's Warbler, Dartford Warbler, Sardinian Warbler, Blackcap, Long-tailed Tit, Crested Tit, Jay, Iberian Magpie, Jackdaw, Spotless Starling, Serin, Linnet, Hawfinch, Cirl Bunting, Rock Bunting

Breeding visitors: Lesser Kestrel, Red-necked Nightjar, Swift, Pallid Swift, Bee-eater, Red-rumped Swallow, Nightingale, Golden Oriole

Non-breeding visitors: Cormorant, Dunnock, Chiffchaff, Firecrest

How to visit it

The old town holds several specialities including a colony of Lesser Kestrels, several pairs of White Stork and some Blue Rock Thrushes. Perhaps one of the best ways to visit it is to follow the road that leads from the centre to the pier at the Guadiana valley (37.6378, -7.6626). At the bottom, it is possible to walk along the edge of the river.

The large bridge over the Guadiana is also a good spot to scan the valley (free parking is available at both ends). Crag Martins are usually present and can be numerous in winter. At the eastern end, a small road to the right leads to a place called Além-Rio. Views over the town are magnificent, and Blue Rock Thrush is often seen here.

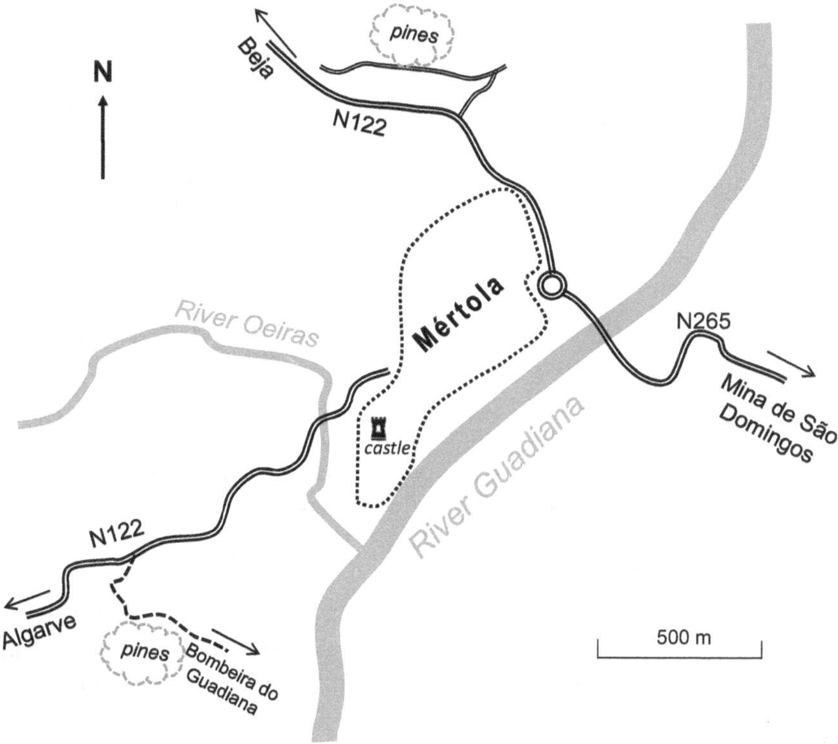

There is another bridge on the western side of the town, over the river Oeiras (37.6381, -7.6666) - this is a good spot for Rock Bunting. Under the bridge, there are nest boxes for Lesser Kestrels.

Another interesting way to explore the Guadiana valley is at Bombeira do Guadiana. To get there, leave Mértola southwards on the N122 and after 800 m look for an unsurfaced road to the left signposted 'Bombeira do Guadiana'. This road crosses some Umbrella Pine plantations, where it is possible to find several forest birds including Crested Tit and Hawfinch, and then along the Guadiana valley. It is a quiet area and offers excellent views over the river and Mértola.

Pulo do Lobo

A deep river valley with a rocky gorge, surrounded by scrub and oak woodland. There are also small reservoirs nearby.

Birds

Resident: Red-legged Partridge, Bonelli's Eagle, Golden Eagle, Griffon Vulture, Cinereous Vulture, Hoopoe, Woodlark, Thekla's Lark, Crag Martin, Grey Wagtail, Blue Rock Thrush, Cetti's Warbler, Sardinian Warbler, Blackcap, Short-toed Treecreeper, Crested Tit, Iberian Magpie, Spotless Starling, Serin, Linnet, Hawfinch, Cirl Bunting, Rock Bunting, Corn Bunting

Breeding visitors: Black Stork, Short-toed Eagle, Little Ringed Plover, Cuckoo, White-rumped Swift, Red-rumped Swallow, Golden Oriole

Non-breeding visitors: Meadow Pipit, Black Redstart, Song Thrush

How to visit it

'Pulo do Lobo' means literally 'The wolf's jump'. The name is a reference to the fact that the River Guadiana is so narrow here that even a wolf can jump it. Two roads lead to this place (one on either side of the river). The western route is described here, as the road is in better condition.

Leave Mértola northwards on the N122 and after 3 km veer right to Corte Gafo. Proceed following signs to Pulo do Lobo, pass through Amendoeira da Serra and follow the road until the tarmac ends and gives way to a dirt road. There is a gate which is often closed, but the passage is allowed (please close the gate after passing through it).

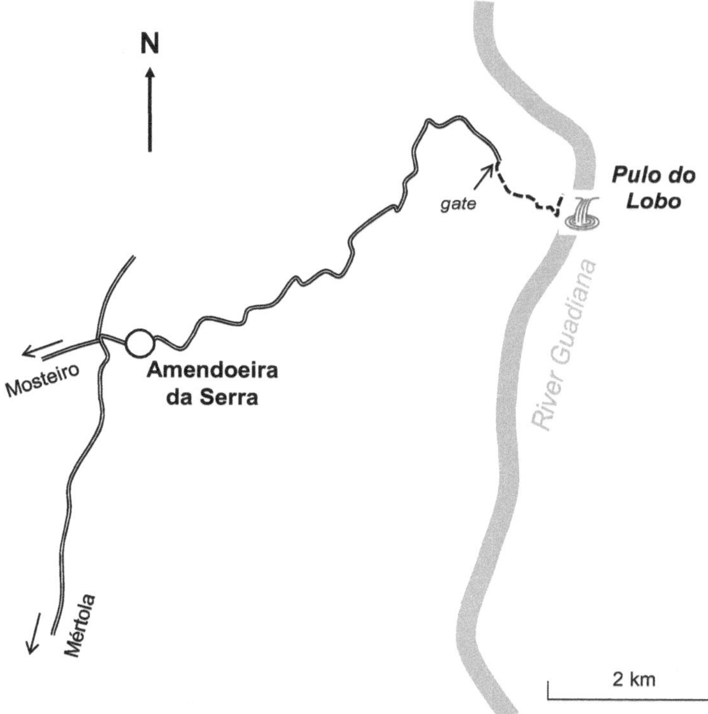

The dirt road goes among Holm Oaks (which have some forest birds), passes near two small reservoirs (that sometimes attract waterbirds) and finally approaches the river. It is possible to park (37.8042, -7.6343) and inspect the valley from the platform. The rocks typically have Blue Rock Thrush and Rock Bunting, while Crag Martins fly around. A look at the sky often produces large soaring birds, including eagles, vultures and Black Stork.

A narrow trail continues northwards along the river and makes it possible to explore that section of the valley.

As mentioned above, it is also possible to approach Pulo do Lobo from the eastern side, namely from the N265 that links Mértola to Serpa.

Mina de São Domingos

An abandoned open-pit mine. The landscape is peculiar, and some ruins of the old buildings still exist.

Birds

Resident: White Stork, Griffon Vulture, Cinereous Vulture, Golden Eagle, Kestrel, Iberian Green Woodpecker, Hoopoe, Thekla's Lark, Crag Martin, Blue Rock Thrush, Dartford Warbler, Sardinian Warbler, Southern Grey Shrike, Iberian Magpie, Spotless Starling, Rock Sparrow, Serin, Linnet, Hawfinch

Breeding visitors: Short-toed Eagle, Little Ringed Plover, Turtle Dove, Cuckoo, Common Swift, White-rumped Swift, Bee-eater, Wryneck, Red-rumped Swallow, Black-eared Wheatear, Golden Oriole, Woodchat Shrike

How to visit it

From Mértola, take the N265 eastwards and follow it for 17 km. Upon arriving at the village called 'Mina de São Domingos', a large reservoir appears on the left. This is called Tapada Grande. Despite its size, it does not attract many waterbirds.

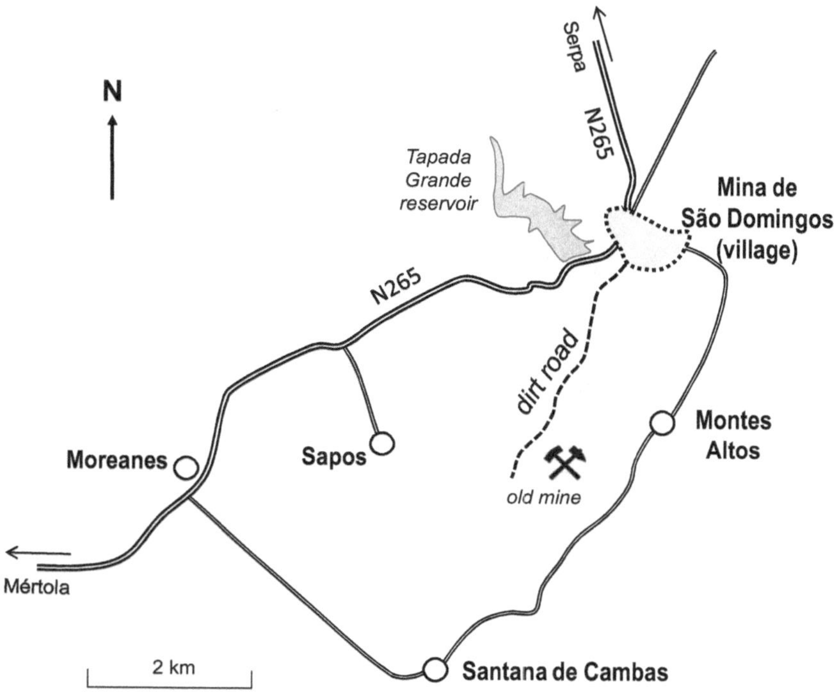

The most interesting route is the dirt road leading to the old mine premises. Leave the N265 and cross the village, following signs to 'Mina-ruínas' or 'Complexo Mineiro' (the signs may not be very obvious – the dirt road starts at 37.6696, -7.4999).

The landscape looks somewhat desolate, and at first sight, there seem to be no birds at all. There is a large amount of debris, which in spring attracts many Black-eared Wheatears. It is worth stopping near the old mine buildings – a careful inspection should provide Crag Martin, Red-rumped Swallow and Blue Rock Thrush. This is also a well-known site for the rare White-rumped Swift – patience is required to see this elusive species, which arrives late and is not usually recorded before May. An early morning visit increases the chances of success.

The surrounding area is covered by several Pine and Eucalyptus plantations. Birds in this habitat include Iberian Green Woodpecker, Iberian Magpie and Golden Oriole.

A look at the sky may produce some raptors. Griffon and Cinereous Vultures do not breed here, but sometimes a few individuals, probably wandering from nearby Spain, fly over this place. Short-toed Eagle is also regular at this location, and Golden Eagle has been recorded.

Pomarão

Deep valleys dominated by scrub, rocky outcrops and a few trees.

Birds

Resident: Red-legged Partridge, Little Egret, Kestrel, Eagle Owl, Kingfisher, Hoopoe, Crag Martin, Wren, Blue Rock Thrush, Cetti's Warbler, Dartford Warbler, Sardinian Warbler, Blackcap, Long-tailed Tit, Jay, Iberian Magpie, Spotless Starling, Spanish Sparrow, Common Waxbill, Serin, Linnet, Hawfinch, Rock Bunting

Breeding visitors: Bee-eater, Red-rumped Swallow, Nightingale, Black-eared Wheatear, Subalpine Warbler, Woodchat Shrike, Golden Oriole,

Non-breeding visitors: Cormorant, Grey Heron, Black-headed Gull, Sandwich Tern, Dunnock, Black Redstart, Song Thrush, Siskin

How to visit it

Access from Mértola is on the N265, veering right after about 5 km. Pass Fernandes and Alves and at the next T-junction take the right road which leads to Pomarão, a tiny village on the left bank of the Guadiana. On the other side of the river lies Mesquita (see page 44).

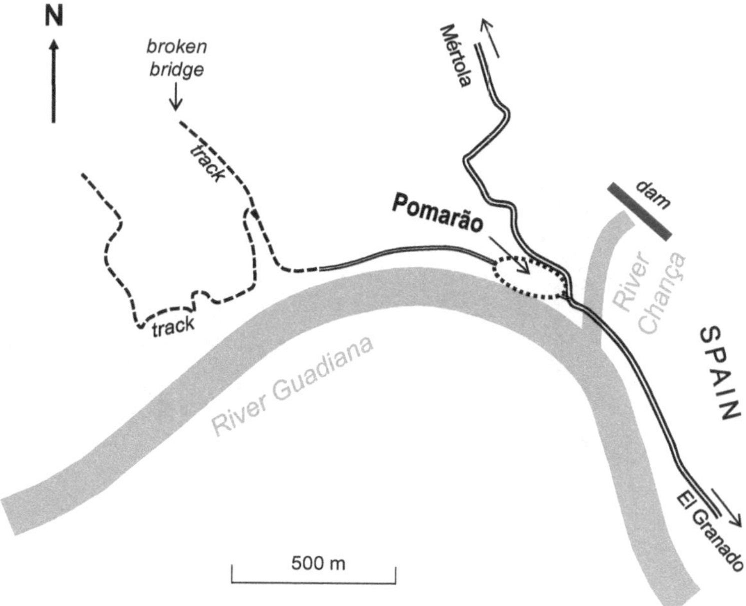

The river doesn't usually have many waterbirds, but it is worth taking a look at it, especially in winter, as sometimes there are herons, gulls or even terns; besides, migratory birds might move through following the course of the river. Cetti's Warbler occurs along the bank, and its song can often be heard. At the southern end of the village, the bridge linking to Spain crosses the river Chança and also deserves inspection.

The large Eucalyptus trees along the shore of the Guadiana attract a few forest birds, notably Long-tailed Tit and Jay, both of which are quite scarce in the region. The village itself has Blue Rock Thrush – look for it in the ruined buildings.

To explore away from the valley, the best approach is to follow the track marked GR15 that leads northwards. This is the course of the old railway line that linked this place to Mina de São Domingos (the old tunnel is still there), and it leads into a narrow, deep valley (37.5586, -7.5358). Eagle Owl is known to occur here but is, as usual, very elusive. Other birds along here include Crag Martin, Blue Rock Thrush (in the rocky outcrops), Hawfinch, Rock Bunting and wintering Dunnock. After a while, the track forks. GR15 goes to the left and uphill. It is possible to continue straight ahead, but after a few hundred metres, the track ends at a broken bridge.

Mesquita

An area of scrub on the right bank of the river Guadiana.

Birds

Resident: Red-legged Partridge, Little Egret, Little Owl, Kingfisher, Hoopoe, Thekla's Lark, Woodlark, Crag Martin, Wren, Stonechat, Cetti's Warbler, Dartford Warbler, Sardinian Warbler, Blackcap, Long-tailed Tit, Southern Grey Shrike, Iberian Magpie, Spotless Starling, Linnet, Hawfinch, Rock Bunting, Corn Bunting, Common Waxbill

Breeding visitors: Turtle Dove, Bee-eater, Red-rumped Swallow, Nightingale, Black-eared Wheatear, Subalpine Warbler, Woodchat Shrike, Golden Oriole

Non-breeding visitors: Great Cormorant, Meadow Pipit, Song Thrush

How to visit it

This is a rather remote and one of the least visited areas in the region - it is located at the southern tip of the Guadiana Valley Natural Park, just across Pomarão (see page 42). Access is through the village of Mesquita, which lies 25 km southeast of Mértola – from this town, follow the N122 southwards for 18 km, then veer left and proceed for another 7 km until Mesquita. At this place (37.5391, -7.5366), the tarmac ends, but it is possible to proceed on unsurfaced wide tracks. Two options are available.

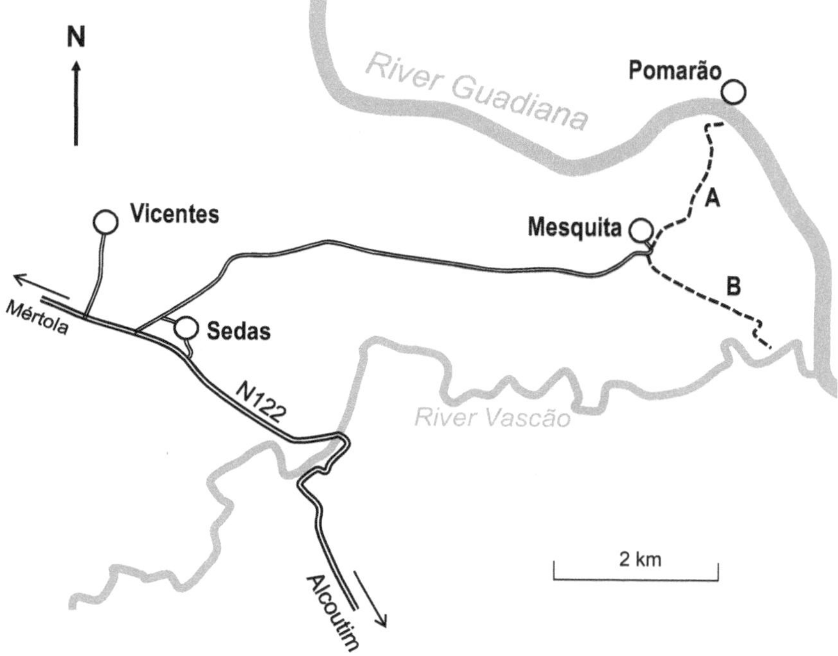

Route A leads to the Guadiana valley and can be done by car. At first, it goes through an area of scrub, where typical birds include Thekla's Lark, Black-eared Wheatear and Dartford Warbler. After a while, it goes steeply downwards, as it approaches the Guadiana. From the bank of the river, one has a nice view of Pomarão. The river has a riparian gallery, mainly willows, and here it is possible to find several passerines, including the exotic Waxbill (not a common bird in this region), Golden Oriole, Long-Tailed Tit and Nightingale. It is also worth taking a look at the river, as waterbirds sometimes turn up.

Route B leads southwards towards the river Vascão (a tributary of the Guadiana). The track is quite rough, so unless you have a four-wheel-drive, it is better to walk. The surrounding hillsides are covered by scrub, mainly Gum Rockrose. Birds here include Thekla's Lark and various *Sylvia* warblers. After a while, the river Vascão appears, as it runs along a deep valley into the Guadiana, which is also visible in the distance. The track starts to go down. This sector is rarely visited by birdwatchers, so some other surprises may occur.

Additional sites

In this section, we suggest a few additional sites that may also be good for birdwatching. Most of them have been included because they are known as reliable places for seeing certain species.

For each of these sites, we provide a brief description and a suggestion on how it can be explored. The coordinates of the main reference points are also given. A general map has been included (page 48).

Castro Verde town

A stop at this town might produce interesting sightings. Breeding visitors include Common and Pallid Swifts. Raptors frequently fly over, including Red and Black Kites, and Booted Eagle. Barn Owl is resident and can sometimes be seen at night flying over the streets. Long-eared Owls are regularly recorded, especially in winter – they roost in the pepper trees, usually near the fire brigade building.

Hortas comunitárias reservoir

A small reservoir next to the N2, close to a few market gardens. The place is fenced off but can be partially seen from the main road (37.7191, -8.0870). This location attracts waterfowl and waders, including Black-winged Stilt. The surrounding plains often have raptors and sometimes steppe birds.

Fontes Bárbaras

This area is located southeast of Carregueiro, between the N2 and the road to Entradas. A track links both roads and can be done by car – its endpoints lie at (37.7602, -8.0949) and (37.7977, -8.0609). This route is about 7 km long, it goes through open country and provides an opportunity to see steppe birds and raptors. In winter, there may be Cranes and Golden Plovers. There is also a reservoir.

Entradas reservoir

Just south of Entradas, next to the minor road leading to São Marcos da Ataboeira, lies another reservoir. This one is very accessible and often has a variety of waterfowl, including Red-crested Pochard. Other species that have been regularly recorded around here include Glossy Ibis, Great Spotted Cuckoo and Black-bellied Sandgrouse. It is possible to park under the Eucalyptus trees (37.7665, -8.0098) and inspect the water body from there.

River Cobres

This small river flows north-eastwards. For many years it has been known as one of the best places to find the Rufous-tailed Scrub Robin. The river can be approached from the road linking Entradas to São Marcos da Ataboeira – there is a bridge at (37.7282, -7.9768).

River Maria Delgada

Another small river, which flows into the river Cobres, mentioned above; it is another good location to look for the Rufous-tailed Scrub Robin. The bridge of the N123 (37.6922, -8.0290) is probably the best place to get close to this valley.

São Pedro das Cabeças

A few km southeast of Castro Verde lies a hill with a chapel on the top. The slopes are covered with scattered Holm Oaks, where Scops Owl can be heard in spring. Slightly to the north, near Geraldos, the bridge over river Maria Delgada (37.6794, -8.0477) also deserves inspection, as it is a good spot for Kingfisher and Crag Martin.

São Marcos da Ataboeira

An area of open country south of the N123, which is another excellent place to find steppe birds, namely Great and Little Bustards, Lesser Kestrel, Black-bellied Sandgrouse, and Roller. It lies a few km east of São Marcos da Ataboeira and can be approached by following a track that starts at (37.7078, -7.9198).

Vale de Açor

Vale de Açor is probably the best location in the entire region to see flocks of wintering Cranes. It lies on the N122, about 25 km northwest of Mértola. About 1 km north of Vale de Açor, look for a track to the left signposted Herdade dos Lagos (37.7988, -7.8585). This track leads to the shore of a reservoir, which is a good place to watch the Cranes. There is another reservoir about 2 km further west, but permission should be sought at the farm to visit it.

Almajões reservoir

A small reservoir a few km east of Mértola and just north of the N265. As with other reservoirs in the region, the number of birds is extremely variable, depending on water levels. Stone Curlew, Collared Pratincole, Red-crested Pochard and Great Reed Warbler have all been recorded here, along with other waterbirds. Access is made on foot from here: (37.6325, -7.6017).

Corvos and Corte Sines

An interesting but little explored area north of the N265, northwest of Moreanes (see map on page 41). At Corvos there is a reservoir (37.6617, -7.6010), which often attracts waterfowl and waders. Golden Eagle has also been recorded here. Corte Sines is located a few km to the north and consists of mixed habitat with oak trees, where it is possible to find some forest birds.

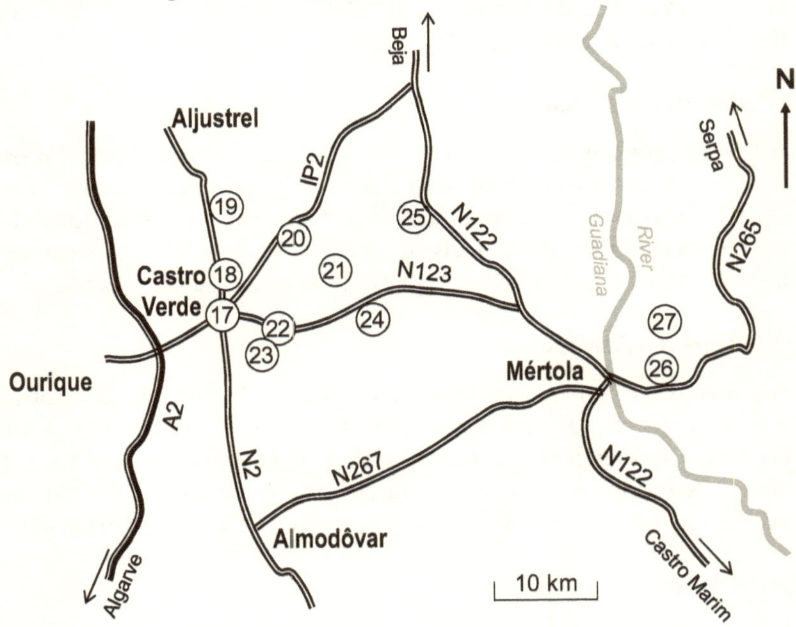

17. Castro Verde
18. Charca das hortas comunitárias
19. Fontes Bárbaras
20. Entradas
21. River Cobres
22. River Maria Delgada
23. São Pedro das Cabeças
24. São Marcos da Ataboeira
25. Vale de Açor
26. Almajões reservoir
27. Corvos and Corte Sines

Map of additional birding sites around Castro Verde and Mértola

About the author

Gonçalo Elias is the author or co-author of twenty books about birds and the best places to watch them, both in English and in Portuguese, including *Guia das Aves de Lisboa, As Aves do Estuário do Tejo, Atlas das Aves Invernantes do Baixo Alentejo, A Birdwatcher's Guide to Portugal, As Aves do Estuário do Sado, Aves de Portugal – Ornitologia do território continental, Birds of Portugal – An Annotated Checklist, Birds of the Algarve and Southern Alentejo*, and *Birding hotspots in the Algarve* (a series of 8 books), along with several papers and notes in specialised ornithological journals.

The author is a founding member of SPEA – Sociedade Portuguesa para o Estudo das Aves (the Portuguese society for the study of birds), and was a member of its board between 1999 and 2002, as well as coordinator of the PRC – the Portuguese Rarities Committee, between 2002 and 2006.

A keen birdwatcher since his teens, Gonçalo Elias has visited over 30 different countries in four continents to watch birds and has participated in nine bird atlases in Portugal, Spain, and Tanzania.

www.ingramcontent.com/pod-product-compliance
Lightning Source LLC
Chambersburg PA
CBHW051422250726
48655CB00003B/1189